UNCOMMON SENSE

LEADERSHIP PRINCIPLES TO GROW YOUR BUSINESS PROFITABLY

THOMAS W. FARANDA

Printed in the United States of America

Printing and Typesetting Services by
TECNICOM of Solon, Ohio

Art & Cover Design by Steve Fuerst
Fuerst Art & Printing, St. Paul, MN

ISBN (International Standard Book Number): 1-877629-02-2

KNOWLEDGE PRESS: 8680 Black Maple Drive
                    Eden Prairie, MN 55344

      (as of 1-1-92)   9790 N. Invergordon
                    Paradise Valley, AZ 85253

Book purchases are available from Knowledge Press.

10 9 8 7 6 5 4 3 2

AUTHOR DEDICATION

Success in every aspect of your personal life and your professional career is inherently related to your attitude toward yourself and toward others.

In life and in work, you are treated in the exact manner in which you allow others to treat you. You determine your own level of self-esteem, your own level of success and your own barriers to a happy and productive life.

> This book is dedicated to people who have learned to respect others just for who and what they are, without imposing their own limits, restrictions, prejudices or expectations on them.
>
> This book is dedicated to people who help others to believe in themselves and to value themselves as important, unique and valuable human beings.
>
> **This book is specifically dedicated to my wife, Cheryl, because she is a partner to be proud of and because she always has believed in me.**

AUTHOR ACKNOWLEDGEMENTS

The author thanks Dr. Peter Drucker, the master who has taught all of us so much about business and leadership.

The author thanks Barry Wisner for his help with the book title, Steven Fuerst for his design ideas, Bob Morris for his marketing expertise, Steve Sabo, Chuck Straka and Norm Schilling for their printing guidance and Pat Kingsley for years of friendship and assistance.

Finally, the author thanks Ross and Sylvia Faranda, his parents, for teaching him about business, life and integrity.

Thomas W. Faranda

> *"Perfection*
> *is beyond humanity.*
>
> *But that does not mean*
> *we should abandon*
> *excellence*
> *as our goal."*

Thomas W. Faranda

As Quoted in *FORBES Magazine*

AUTHOR FORWARD

I have never been sure if I am more interested in the philosophy of business or the business of philosophy.

This book is a combination of both philosophy and business. It is a practical view of the most critical aspects of life and business as both are intertwined.

The intent of the book is to provide guidance and direction to supervisors, managers, business owners and all professionals related to the business community. At the same time, the book is designed to provide a philosophical view of life and business with an edge toward the humor that drives both life and business.

This book is simply an organized renewal of the ideas and philosophy that have helped people become happier and more successful in their careers and their lives.

This book is light and airy and simple. Yet, like all truly simple things, it is profoundly impactful. It is filled with simple things, simple concepts, simple directions. These simplicities, when well executed, will enrich your career and your life.

The choice of what to do with the Faranda Maxims is yours.

You can choose to read the Maxims and simply enjoy them. Or, you can choose to read them and act to put them to work for you. Without action on your part the Maxims will be great entertainment. With action, the Maxims will help you to change your life.

I wish you happiness, health and harmony.
I wish you wisdom, warmth and wealth.
I wish you action.

Thomas W. Faranda

<u>SPREAD THE PETALS GENTLY</u>

*The most beautiful part of
a flower is the part
we see the least of.*

*But it is there...
Hidden amidst the petals,
Waiting to open,
to be warmed,
to be noticed.*

*People are like flowers...
Spread the petals gently.*

THOMAS W. FARANDA

As Published In
Our Twentieth Centuries Greatest Poems,
World of Poetry Press, 1982, Sacramento, CA.

INTRODUCTION

By Mr. N. Krishnan

Distributor of the India Edition of UNCOMMON SENSE
and Executive Director of
Creative Communications & Management Center, Bombay.

Thomas Faranda is a remarkable personality. He has earned an international reputation in the management field in practically all the continents. He has major world corporations such as IBM, 3M, Siemens and General Electric as his clients. He was a candidate for the United States Senate in 1988. He has worked in Japan, Saudi Arabia, India, Singapore, Africa, throughout Europe, America and many additional areas of the world.

The bare essentials of good management are commonsense and leadership. Yet, commonsense is very often not so commonly found. The maxims in this book are replete with uncommon commonsense. The author's maxims are laid forth in a truly remarkable style, a class of authorship difficult to surpass.

Reading even a single Faranda Maxim is like being prescribed an elixir for healthy management. Some of them articulate general truths. Some of them carry advice and admonition in good measure. Some of them are epigrams with an impact while some have a telling pithiness about them. Some of them are succinctly profound and a few are mildly shocking while they demolish a few management shibboleths. Finally, some of the aphorisms read like a tried and tested panacea for management ills.

The Faranda Maxims on 'Leadership' and 'Management' provide modern insights into ancient problems. All of this can only emanate from a management scholar of Thomas Faranda's caliber.

There is hidden wisdom throughout this book. I invite you to open UNCOMMON SENSE and read a remarkable book from a remarkable personality.

Mr. N. Krishnan

> *"The Greatest*
> *Revolution...*
> *Is the discovery*
> *that human beings,*
> *by changing*
> *the inner attitudes*
> *of their minds.*
> *Can change*
> *the outer aspects*
> *of their lives."*
>
> WILLIAM JAMES

CONTENTS

> **FARANDA MAXIM**
>
> *The Best People*
> *Always Leave First.*
> *The Worst People*
> *Never Leave.*

The Leader's Job is to Recruit, Hire, Reward, and Retain the Best People.

The best people know they are good and can get another job any time they choose.

The worst people know they are not good and that no one will hire them if they leave.

Thus, the best people leave when they do not get the rewards of effective leadership and recognition they feel they deserve.

When they leave, they go to work for your competition. The worst people remain to take their positions.

The leader's job is to insure that the best people never leave.

The leader's job is to help the worst people to relocate to the competition.

A
ATTITUDE

FARANDA MAXIM

Surround yourself with Nutritious people. Non-nutritious people Are takers not givers. They suck out your soul.

Invest Your Time With People Who Lead You to Success!

Nutritious people provide energy, vitality, motivation and joy.

Nutritious people are givers not takers.

Nutritious people empower you with a will to win and a belief in yourself. They help you to reach new plateaus of personal accomplishment and professional success.

Nutritious people help you to expand your limits.

Surround yourself with nutritious people and you will grow successful together.

> **FARANDA MAXIM**
>
> *A winning philosophy is paramount to success. "You can't win them all" is paramount to failure.*

Believing in Yourself and in Your Success is Paramount to Winning.

You must go in believing you can and will win. This positive belief sets up a positive mindset and gives you an edge on your competition.

Leaders who go into the race saying "you can't win them all" are probably right. It's called the "pygmalion effect" – you become what you think you are or are not.

To believe in your success, you must live by a strong ethical and moral philosophy.

Without a philosophy, a person is like an empty ravioli – all dough and no go.

Be a whole ravioli. Develop your philosophy. Stuff yourself. (Whole raviolis have more fun!)

A

ATTITUDE

FARANDA MAXIM

The "Black Spot Syndrome"

*We always see
the black spot...
and
We miss all
the white space
around it!*

Learn to Focus on Your Strengths, Not Your Weaknesses.

When we look in the mirror we instantly focus on the one part of our body we dislike the most and we miss all the beautiful parts around it.

When we read the daily newspaper we instantly focus on the negative rather than the positive – negative news sells newspapers. We forget all the joy in the world.

"214 people died today in the plane crash in Denver" (negative).
"200,000 people today had a successful flight" (positive).

Learn to focus yourself on the positive aspects of life. Learn to focus on your strengths, not your weaknesses.

Negative attitudes, negative self-image and negative self-talk have never made a successful leader or person.

Learn to focus on your boss's strengths, your spouse's strengths, other people's strengths. Relationships are never successfully developed by focusing on weaknesses. Relationships are developed by focusing on strengths and on positive mutual benefits.

FARANDA MAXIM

Features "Tell"
Benefits "Sell"

"What's it Mean to Me?"
This is the Most Important Phrase in
Selling.

In the history of the world, no one has ever purchased a product or service on the basis of its features.

People buy benefits and values.

People buy products and services based on what the products and services will do for them.

People, for example, do not care about gas mileage. What people care about is saving money on gas. So, learn to ask the right questions and explain things in the right manner. For example, if you were selling a vehicle . . .

Question: How many miles per gallon do you get right now?

Answer: Twelve miles per gallon

Question: How much money do you spend every month on gas?

Answer: $300

Benefit: Do you realize that the vehicle you are considering gets twenty-four miles per gallon? *What that means to you is* that you will only spend $150 per month on gas. Therefore, you will save $150 per month on gas! (That means you will save $250 gross income dollars per month – the amount you would need to earn to end up with the $150 you would have spent on goods.)

People buy benefits and values, not features. Learn to sell benefits!

Professionals and leaders sell benefits and values, not features. That's why they so often get what they go after!

B

BANKING

Bankers Respond to the Moment – When Your P&L is Strong, Go For It.

An effective leader looks ahead, identifies problems that could occur and finds ways to stop the problem from occurring.

Financial problems top the list.

An effective leader makes a partner out of a banker – an advisor rather than an adversary.

An effective leader brings a strong P&L to the banker and arranges a line of credit before he/she needs it. They never wait until they need the money to ask for it.

When you do not need money, banks will solicit you to take money. When you really do need money, most banks seem to disappear. The best banks – the leaders – do not disappear when you need them. They have learned that solving problems for their customers builds relationships that pay off in the long term.

Banks do not like to give away money. They like to invest it. They like to get it back.

If you cannot prove your ability to re-pay it, they will not give it to you. All of us have times when we do not look like we can re-pay it. Ask for it when you look like you can repay it.

This system works much better.

Remember, always arrange for money when you don't need it.

> **FARANDA MAXIM**
>
> *A consultant is a person who will charge you to tell you what your own people would have told you for free...*
> *If you asked and listened!*

Do Not Use Consultants as a Substitute for Talking to Your Own People Yourself.

Use consultants to teach you how to talk to your own people.

Use consultants to help you solve a problem which is beyond your expertise.

Use consultants to help you in a specific technical area for which you have no "in-house" staff.

Use consultants to act as "third-party independents" when you need a fresh look at things.

Use consultants for anything and everything as long as you are not using them to hide from your own people.

Learn to use consultants wisely and you will benefit in personal growth, professional ability and ROI.

A consultant used correctly is an investment, not a cost.

C

CONTROL

Learn to Inspect What you Expect

Control is the Process of Comparing What Should Have Been Done With What Has Been Done.

Control requires you to ask why there is a difference between what was expected and what was accomplished.

Control demands that you identify and fix the problem – the difference between what was expected and what was accomplished.

The world is littered with good people who failed to set standards and goals for themselves or who failed to ask themselves "Why?" when they did not reach their goals.

The world is littered with good companies who failed to set standards and goals or failed to monitor their results based on those standards and goals.

International Harvestor, People Express and many other firms are examples of organizations who have failed to use effective control. Today these firms are either bankrupt or have gone through major reorganization to try to survive.

Don't go bankrupt.

Set standards and goals. Monitor them. Ask the "Why?" question. When there is a problem, fix it.

> FARANDA MAXIM
>
> *The amount a person uses his/her imagination... Is inversely proportional to the amount of punishment he/she receives for using it!*

People Do That for Which They are Rewarded.

A child who is punished (or simply not rewarded) for using his/her imagination and creativity will become an uncreative adult.

A child who is rewarded (or simply recognized) for using his/her imagination and creativity will become a creative adult.

Uncreative people seldom succeed or prosper in today's world.

Creative people prosper today because they have the ability of "discovery" – the ability to look at the same thing as everyone else and think something different.

Polaroid cameras came from the mind of the three year old daughter of Dr. Edward Land, the founder of Polaroid.

Post-it notes came from the mind of a scientist at 3M Corporation because he looked at a problem and saw an opportunity.

Velcro came from the mind of a Scottish scientist who took the time to look at a common wood burr under a microscope.

Creativity is a main ingredient to success and happiness in life and in work.

Let the kid in you out.

Learn to use your creativity. You will live a happier and more prosperous life.

C
COMMUNICATION

The Old Philosophy "Do What I Say, Not What I Do" is Dead.

Today, people assume that they can do whatever you – the leader – does. Your ability to be an effective role model depends on your ability to set a good example.

If you do not want people to lie, cheat, steal, come in late, not come in, take long breaks and so on ... don't do it yourself.

Remember another Faranda Maxim – "Employees always know everything before management."

Anything you do or say will be known. If you do not want it to be known, don't do it or say it. If you have to do it or say it, make sure you do so with absolute discretion.

Remember, as a leader you are always "on stage."

Leadership is what you do or don't do, what you say or don't say. Leadership is setting a positive example and being an effective role model.

Leadership is an art as well as a science. Be an artist and you'll be a leader. Be a scientist and you'll be a manager.

An effective leader/manager is an artist and a scientist.

What was isn't any more.
What is won't be for long!

C
CHANGE

Ninety-eight Percent of all the Significant Change in the History of the World Has Occurred in the Last Lifetime.

The pace of change in the western world has been staggering. In the last lifetime of seventy-five years, people have gone from dying of appendicitis to surviving heart and lung transplants.

In the last lifetime, people have experienced transportation from five mph on foot, to twenty-five mph by car, to six hundred mph by jet airplane. We have military jets that fly at Mach 2 and space shuttles that travel at sixty thousand miles per hour.

The pace of change is increasing.

In the next lifetime of seventy-five years, there will be more changes again than ever in the history of mankind.

Change is a positive as well as a painful process.

Change destroys structure, but builds technology. Societies are often destroyed by decaying structures and usually developed by evolving technologies.

Leaders learn to live with and utilize change as a stepping stone to success in their personal and professional lives.

Learn to live with change, or it will kill you.

C

CHANGE

FARANDA MAXIM

The best way to cope with change... is to create it!

Weak Leaders React to Change.
Strong Leaders Create Change.

People and organizations, like cookies, get stale over time.

Open up the windows and let fresh air in. Although you will get dust, you will also get the sparkling freshness of new ideas.

Change can be viewed as an enemy or a friend.

Successful people and organizations choose to view change as a friend. They use it to grow and succeed.

Sometimes you get mad at a friend. But he/she still remains your friend. Sometimes getting mad makes you think from a different perspective. This is healthy. Learn to thank your friend.

Change is not your enemy unless you choose to make it your enemy.

Change is growth.

Change is life.

Relish it.

Live it.

Create it.

*Leaders who fail to send
a clear signal...
Are "Tuned Out"!*

Learn to Communicate to Express and Not to Impress.

Nothing is more important to a leader than effective communication skills.

The best decision-makers are seldom effective unless they can communicate their decisions effectively to the people who make the decisions work.

Communication is the tool that allows people to buy into the leader's ideas. If people do not buy into the program, the program will fail.

Churchill learned to communicate effectively although he was born with a speech impediment. He corrected it. He knew he could never be an effective leader unless he could communicate with impact. He learned to use simple words. He called them "words that people know."

Today's leaders have learned to speak in "sound bites!" These are short phrases with only one central idea. They are easily understood. They are effective. Learn to use this technique.

Communication is a skill based tool. To be effective as a communicator you must study to learn the skill and then practice applying the skill. Nothing replaces practice to master effective communication.

Practice sending a clear signal – one central idea that is easily understood. If you fail to send a clear signal you will be tuned out. People only buy into a program or an idea if they believe in it. It is your job to get them to believe in it by sending them a clear signal.

C
COMMUNICATION

Rumors are Usually Worse than Reality!

A good leader communicates frequently, directly and honestly with his/her people.

A good leader does not allow rumor to cloud reality.

What is real is what people <u>think</u> is real.

Perception is reality.

Rumor shapes perception when truth does not. Perception shapes reality as "they" see it.

A good leader stays ahead of the rumor mill by communicating effectively at the right time, in the right place and in the right way.

Poor communication is worse than no communication. Poor communication twists perceptions into false realities. It generates rumors.

It is better not to communicate at all than to communicate poorly.

It is best to communicate effectively and insure that perception is indeed reality.

>
> *Never break customers'*
> *Buying habits...*
> *Unless they are not*
> *Buying from you!*

Habit is One of Our Most Powerful Buying Motives.

The power of habit is well documented.

People drive to work the same way every day. People sit in the same seats. People visit in the same groups. People buy most of their purchases on the basis of habit.

To change people's buying habits, you must first create dissatisfaction with what they have. Then you must offer them a better alternative.

You create dissatisfaction by demonstrating that your product or service meets their needs and has value to them. No one purchases anything on the basis of features. People only purchase on the basis of benefits and values to them.

You offer your customers a better alternative by knowing them so well that you know what they need and want. Then you demonstrate the value and benefit to them so they understand it. Then they will purchase it.

No one wanted post-it notes. Now everyone wants them. 3M Corporation created dissatisfaction and then offered people a better alternative. Post-its may soon be a $600 million business from an idea no one knew they wanted. 3M Corporation is very pleased. You can live on $600 million.

C

CUSTOMERS

In Today's Business Environment, Everyone Always Wants the "Best" Customers – the Ones that Order Frequently and Pay Promptly.

We live in a competitive world where there are no "trade areas." With "800" phone numbers, instant worldwide communication, multiple suppliers of everything and almost instant delivery, we can do business with anyone who meets our needs and wants.

Customers who order regularly and pay promptly are on the "hit list" of everyone in the industry. They are always bombarded with offers of special terms and special service.

These customers can and do choose a selected list of vendors to do business with. The vendors they choose must provide personalized and effective service, market (or below-market) pricing, intimate knowledge of the customers' business and an "old friend" relationship based on commitment and mutual trust.

Everyone wants these customers. Not everyone deserves them.

To deserve these customers you must commit yourself to excellence and prove your worth over a period of time.

To deserve these customers you must honor a code of ethics and never break your word (or the "spirit" of your word) to your customer.

To deserve these customers you must earn them.

See to your own house, then see to theirs.

> FARANDA MAXIM
>
> *Customers do not want*
> *Your products and services.*
> *Customers only want*
> *Their needs and wants met!*

A Customer is Not Interested in What a Product or Service Will Do For <u>You</u>. They Only Care What It Will Do For <u>Them</u>!

All business must be directed to your customers' needs and wants.

Customers are buying solutions to their problems. Customers are buying satisfaction of their needs. Customers are buying gratifications of their wants. Customers are buying pain and problem removal.

Customers are buying your ability to give them these things.

Customers can find what they want without you. Your goal is to get them to find what they want from you and not from your competition.

To get them to buy from you means you must make a commitment to know their needs and wants so well that you can anticipate them. You must know their business so well that you are considered part of their team. You must build long-term, trusting relationships with your customers.

In the future, customers will buy from a smaller number of vendors. The vendors will be part of the "team" because they will have developed close, long-term relationships based on trust and commitment.

Today is the day to start building your customer relationships.

Without great customer relationships you have no future.

C
CUSTOMERS

Your best customers are your Present Customers

Treat Your Customers Like Gold In Your Safe Deposit Box!

Present customers should be valued and not ignored. Too often we search for new customers and new target markets and we forget the customers who made us successful.

Sears learned this lesson in the 1970's. Sears looked to the upper middle class as their market of the future. They poured all their resources into this market at the expense of their traditional lower middle class market. After a few years (and a few hundred million dollars) Sears realized this "market of the future" didn't want them. When they tried to return to their traditional market they found out they didn't want them anymore either. Their market had been "wooed" away by K-Mart, Target, Wal-Mart and others.

This is a hard way to learn a simple lesson. Your best customers are your present customers

People Express didn't learn anything from Sears. In the search for new markets and new customers they forgot their present customers. So, their customers forgot them. People Express, a $1 billion company, no longer exists.

Past customers can be converted to present customers. Sometimes all it takes is a phone call from a sincere person who asks them to come back. Ask them why they stopped doing business with you. Ask them what you can do to help them. Tell them you value their business and want them back. Prove it by knowing their business. Many of them will give you a second chance. Don't blow it.

If you mess up the second chance, they will not only stop doing business with you, they will try to bury you. People are forgiving once and forewarned twice. Then they get vicious.

> ### FARANDA MAXIM
>
> *What you do To or For*
> *Your customers*
> *Is the difference between*
> *Success and Failure.*

Business and Leadership Success is the Result of What You Do To or For Your Customers.

McDonalds Corporation spent over a million dollars developing their theme, "We do it all for you." They meant it. They did it.

McDonalds Corporation earned over a billion dollars from their theme, "We do it all for you."

The key word is "for."

If we change one word of the McDonalds slogan we get a totally different feeling about the company and the product.

"We do it all to you" just doesn't sound the same, does it?

What you do to or for your customers will determine your leadership and business success.

It's totally up to you. Write the slogan any way you choose. Then, learn to live with the results.

"We do it all for you" should be enshrined as one of life's great success secrets. It works for products, services, people and leaders.

C

CREDIT

Until We Collect the Money, All We Have is a Cost!

We spend thousands of dollars to locate target markets and to advertise to them. We continue spending thousands of dollars to put a professional sales force in the field to personally call on prospects and customers.

Then we try to save a few dollars by maintaining an understaffed credit management department.

Only recently have some organizations started to realize the critical importance of effective credit management. These organizations are the successful ones. They understand the golden rules:

- Credit management is an investment, not a cost.
- Don't count the money until it is in your hot little hand.

Credit management requires well selected, well-trained professionals who are experts in their chosen field. This is not the place to save a few dollars or to "cut back" as soon as sales slow down. This is the place that provides the final link in the organization's cash flow and survival.

No one pays enough attention to the credit people until the cash flow dries up.

It's time we gave proper credit to our credit people as a critical part of the team.

Leaders know that their credit team turns the handles on the financial faucets: treat them as professionals and you'll never run out of hot water.

> FARANDA MAXIM
>
> *Discovery*
> *Is looking at the same*
> *Thing as everyone else...*
> *And thinking something*
> *Different!*

Discovery is an "Ah Ha." (An "Oh Heck" is an "Ah Ha" Too Late)

- Polaroid's instant picture camera
- 3M's post-it notes
- Nike's funny looking "waffle sole" shoes
- Crays "super computer"
- Velcro, Xerography, cellular phones, fax machines ...

What these organizations and products all have in common is discovery. They all looked at the same thing as everyone else, but saw something different.

Then they turned the "something different" into a viable and saleable product for the market.

People have the opportunity to see things in their own unique way. Many of us create the ideas, but few of us have the persistence and audacity to bring them successfully to market.

Resources can be found for the right product or service, but discovery must take place first to create the right product or service.

Discovery is not a covert operation. Learn to use and trust your intuition and creativity and the process of discovery will open to you.

As Sherlock Holmes said to Dr. Watson, "You see, Dr. Watson, but you do not observe."

Learn to observe as a prelude to discovery.

Discovery pays.

D

DECISION
MAKING

Never let a subordinate
Come to you
with a problem.
Make him/her
come to you with
Three to five solutions
to the problem.

The Decision Makers' Responsibility is Not Just to Make the Decision. It is to Teach Others to Make the Decision.

When you allow a subordinate to come to you with a problem, you do not allow him/her the growth opportunity to learn to define and solve the problem.

When you require a subordinate to define the problem and to develop three to five possible solutions to the problem, you are helping the person to develop skills.

You are acting as a catalyst to their future success.

You are providing role modeling and leadership. You are assisting the development of creative thinking as applied to decision making and problem solving.

People cannot grow and develop without the skills of decision making and problem solving. Help them to grow. Allow them to think and create. Support them in their decisions so they will learn to take responsibility and to grow from their mistakes as well as their successes.

No one wants to promote a loser. A loser is a person who has not learned to make effective decisions.

Tomorrow's leaders will be effective teachers. Help develop a leader today – for tomorrow.

> FARANDA MAXIM
>
> *Delegating motivates*
> *While it trains.*
> *Delegating goes right to*
> *The bottom line.*

The Sign of an Effective Leader is How Well He/She Delegates to Other People.

The role of an effective leader is to get things done.

The best leaders use the talents of their people to the maximum level. They push their subordinates to learn and grow. They care enough about their people to really train them in the school of responsibility.

Delegating shows your subordinates that you trust and respect them. Delegating forces people to learn and accept responsibility.

Only a weak leader will not delegate.

Weak leaders like to be surrounded by weak people. Weak leaders favor security and loyalty over progress. They favor mediocrity over excellence.

Develop yourself as a strong leader.

Teach yourself to delegate. Then teach others. You cannot succeed without delegating. You cannot succeed without teaching critical leadership skills to others.

D
DIFFERENTIATION

In Japan, the Nail that is Sticking Up Gets Hammered Down. In America, the Nail that is Not Sticking Up Never Gets Noticed.

The difference between an extraordinary performance and an ordinary performance is not an exceptionally large difference.

In baseball, the difference between a .333 hitter and a .250 hitter is just one more hit in ten times at bat.

In the 1976 Olympic 100 metres dash, the difference between the gold medal winner and the last place finisher was only 1/2 second.

In an ordinary performance there is an extraordinary effort that makes the critical difference between good and great. Somehow the individual pulls an extra burst of energy, creativity or desire from deep within his/her soul.

Great races are seldom won physically. They are won mentally.

Remember that you are in a great race with yourself to achieve your goals and to maximize your potential.

Go for the gold. Strive to be extraordinary.

Being extraordinary will differentiate you from others.

The Japanese say, "the nail that is sticking up gets hammered down." In America make sure your nail is sticking up so that it gets noticed.

> FARANDA MAXIM
>
> *The amount of*
> *differentiation*
> *Your Product/Service has*
> *Is inversely proportional*
> *To the amount of*
> *substitutability it has.*

In Today's World, Everything is Substitutable.

The more substitutability your product, your service or you have in the marketplace, the harder it is to be successful.

You must find ways to differentiate your product, your service or yourself from everyone else. You must develop a distinct market image and presence that people remember and demand.

Ivory soap did it by making a soap that "floated."

Nintendo did it by being a game, not a computer.

Apple did it by making a "personal" computer.

Charmin did it by being "squeezably soft."

Arm & Hammer baking soda did it by becoming a household maintenance product as well as a cooking ingredient.

What is your "USP" – your unique selling proposition? Why are you different? Why should people buy your product or service instead of the competition? What does it mean to them? How are you unique?

Until you can answer these and other questions, you will always be "just another frisbe."

Find a way to differentiate your product or service so it has less substitutability and more market image. Get people to demand your product or service and refuse to accept a substitute.

E

EMPLOYEES

Employees Always Know Everything Before Management.

Learn to Communicate With Your People. They Will Amaze You With What You Do Not Know.

Consultants are hired to talk to your people and tell you what is going on. The reason they are so effective is that consultants often understand this maxim better than managers.

In modern America, nothing is a secret and no subject is taboo. People observe everything and they talk about it openly.

Learn to use your employees as a source of information. Learn to listen to them as a guidepost to knowing what is happening in your own organization.

Employees always know everything first.

The secret is to know how to get them to talk to you about it. The secret is to have a relationship that encourages them to talk to you about it.

Information is power. Employees have information.

Use it in a positive manner to help your organization.

> ### FARANDA MAXIM
>
> *"Perfection*
> *Is beyond humanity...*
> *But that does not mean*
> *We should abandon*
> *Excellence*
> *As our Goal."*

The Pursuit of Excellence Leads to Productivity. The Pursuit of Perfection Leads to Frustration.

It is not cost effective or profitable as a rule to seek perfection. Only specific technological and medical developments demand perfection.

Most products and services only make money when they are excellent but not perfect.

An excellent computer with the appropriate technology, market and price will sell and be profitable. To upgrade an "excellent" computer to a "perfect" computer will affect the market and the price to an extent that it will never be saleable or profitable.

IBM products are sometimes called "inferior but marketable." They are excellent, but not perfect. They have reputation, image and marketing power. They are backed by the best service available. IBM is profitable. It is also one of the world's largest and most successful companies.

Customers demand excellence. They do not demand perfection.

E
EXCELLENCE

It is better to aim for
Excellence
And miss
Than to aim lower and hit.

Aim at Excellence and Create a "Tone" of Excellence Throughout Your Entire Organization.

The "tone" of excellence is a blend of optimism, enthusiasm, vigor, excitement and success.

The "tone" of excellence fosters higher self-esteem and builds self-image in individuals.

The "tone" of excellence helps people develop loyalty and teamwork within the group.

Striving for something better helps people to believe in themselves and in the organization. It helps people believe in challenge and in success. It helps people believe in the people above them who represent "management."

Develop a "tone" of excellence and watch it spread.

Excellence is like a perfect rainbow – it shines over everyone as it frames the sky.

You have to look for a rainbow, but when you find it, it is magic.

> FARANDA MAXIM
>
> *Experience*
> *Is not an asset...*
> *In Time of Rapid*
> *Technological*
> *And Sociological Change*

During Periods of Rapid Change ...
What Was is Less Important Than What
Will Be!

The computer technology of the 1960's is not a factor in today's computer world.

Yesterday's technology is not even a guidepost to help plan tomorrow's technology because the entire basis of the technology has changed and is no longer relevant.

A computer chip today has no resemblance to the transistor of yesterday. The computer chip of today may soon have no resemblance to the "chip" of tomorrow. There may not even be a computer "chip" as we know it today.

During times of rapid change, an effective leader's role is to be ahead of the crowd – to anticipate what the future holds without being tied to the past.

Steven Jobs, one of the founders of Apple Computer, is an effective design engineer because he is not an engineer. He is effective because his focus is on what can be done, rather than what cannot be done or what has been done. The "laws of engineering" mean very little to him – they are simply not relevant to his world.

Seymour Cray jumped two generations of computer technology when he designed the Cray "super computer." He looked at what could be and not at what was.

All successful leaders have learned to use their "experience" to visualize what can be and not what is.

E

EDUCATION

> *Education Teaches You Concepts. Experience Teaches You Skills.*

Experience is the Critical Difference Between Knowing What to Do (Education) and Having Done It (Skill).

Business schools do not teach you how to do business.
(Japan does not have any "business schools")

Law schools do not teach you how to practice law.
(Two-thirds of the world lawyers are in America)

Education is a door-opener, a background preparation, a demonstration of persistence and a necessity. It is not a guarantee of success in your life or your career.

Experience teaches you how to perform these skills with accuracy and excellence.

Skill based knowledge requires experience to yield excellence and success. Experience requires continuous learning over a lifetime to stay "current."

A dull axe, no matter how high the quality, will always lose out to a sharp axe.

Be a sharp axe ... and make your education work for you.

> ### FARANDA MAXIM
> ## *The World is Changing Too Fast...*
> ## *For Those Who are Changing Too Slow!*

The Ability to Adapt is the Truest Test of a Person's Intelligence.

The academic definition of intelligence is the "person's inherent ability to learn." Yet we all know people with great inherent ability and no success.

The medical definition of intelligence is the "person's ability to adapt." We all know people of average "intelligence" who have grown to great personal and business success. The key word is "adapt." Adapt is a synonym for success.

We live in a world where 98% of all significant change in the world has occurred in the last lifetime.

We live in a world where in the last lifetime we have gone . . .

 . . . From dying of appendicitis to heart/lung transplants
 . . . From 5 mph transportation by foot power to 600 mph plane power
 . . . From local communication to instant worldwide communication
 . . . From survival standards of living to rich standards of living.

A shark is one of our world's oldest life forms because of its ability to adapt to its environment. Dinosaurs are extinct.

You have a choice.

Watch the world pass you by, and become extinct. Or, adapt and become successful.

Successful people tend to live healthier and longer lives.

F

FUTURE

A Great Deal of the Knowledge We Need to Know in the Future is Not Even Known Yet.

People who are "learners" always pass people who are "learned."

Learners never learn enough. They see learning as a way of life – a process, not a goal.

If you continue to learn every day you will still never keep up to all of the new knowledge that is developed every day in the world. But you will still be far ahead of almost everyone else.

Knowledge and information often separate those who are making it from those who are "going" to make it.

Learn to read and study as a way of life rather than as a goal to achieve a certain degree or job. The world passes by those who stop learning and participating.

Life is always interesting.

You will not be unless you continue to make yourself so.

Be a "learner," not a "learned."

> **FARANDA MAXIM**
>
> *Tomorrow*
> *Always Arrives Before*
> *You are Ready for it.*

No One is Totally Prepared for the Future but the Best Leaders are Always Preparing.

Tomorrow is never as comfortable as yesterday.

Tomorrow is always a mystery. Yesterday is always a fact.

Some leaders look upon the mystery with fear and dread. Successful leaders look upon it with excitement and adventure.

What you did yesterday is history. It is set in stone and cannot be altered or explained away.

What you are doing today is a moment away from yesterday.

What you do tomorrow can be changed in any way that you wish. You control your own destiny. You are totally responsible for your choices.

Give up yesterday. Accept today. Embrace tomorrow. Tomorrow is your destiny.

F

FLEXIBILITY

FARANDA MAXIM

Learn to Bend
Or
You will Break

I'll Take a Rubber Raft Anyday!

No one runs the Colorado river in a canoe.

A canoe is stiff and unbending and macho, but the river always wins.

The river is unforgiving and unyielding. It breaks anything that refuses to bend.

A raft floats over obstacles and bends to conform to the rapids. It always makes it to the finish line.

Learn to bend or you will learn to break.

Learn to build floating foundations. Even the strongest metal foundations will break under the extreme stresses of an earthquake. But a floating foundation will ride above the shock waves and will still be intact after the last quiver from within the earth.

A floating foundation works because it was created to bend a little. To be flexible. . . .

Successful people are very flexible people.

Flexibility is a key component of the new macho.

If you break, what good are you anymore?

FARANDA MAXIM

The Ability to Follow Precedes The Ability to Lead!

A Good Follower Uses The Experience As a Graduate School Of Leadership.

Effective leaders are not born, they are developed.

Leadership skills can be learned, and if practiced, can be applied with great results.

Winston Churchill, who saved England with the power of his leadership during WWII, is considered to be one of the most powerful speakers of this century. Winston Churchill was born with a speech defect.

He knew he had to conquer his speech defect if he was to develop his leadership skills. He conquered his speech defect. He developed his leadership skills. He mastered the concept of Followership as a Graduate School of Leadership.

Winston Churchill helped save England by learning that no one succeeds as an effective leader until he/she has first succeeded as an effective follower.

In Japan, "Followership" is an honor equal to leadership.

Learn to use Followership as a Graduate School of Leadership.

G
GOALS

Big Shots Are Little Shots That keep Shooting

Very Few Successful People Make It On Their First Attempt. Very Few Successful People Quit Trying to Make It.

Col. Sanders was over retirement age when he finally turned his Kentucky Fried Chicken into a success.

Frank Sinatra used to ask bands to let him sing free while he practiced his craft.

Kermit Wilson started with one hotel, an idea and a vision. He ended up with a chain of Holiday Inns around the world.

F. W. Woolworth went bankrupt numerous times before he finally succeeded with his chain of Woolworth's stores.

R. Macey failed six times before Macey's became a success.

All successful people have a goal, a vision and persistence.

All successful people continue to try until they reach their dream.

> "Everyone is a self-made person.
> Only the successful will admit it."
> Author Unknown

Keep shooting. Re-load when you run out of shells.

Eventually you will hit your target.

Then you'll hit your bull's-eye.

> FARANDA MAXIM
>
> *You Can't Go Wrong*
> *Hiring Right.*
> *You Can't Go Right*
> *Hiring Wrong.*

Good People are the Foundation of All Successful Organizations.

When you hire a person you directly impact the culture and success of the entire organization. Hiring is the most critical, most dangerous and most significant organizational function.

Do it right the first time.

The world is littered with organizations that have failed because they chose the wrong people.

Your customers judge you by the people who work for you.

Always spend whatever amount of time you need to hire the right person the first time.

The right person, at the right time, doing the right job makes a successful organization.

People are an investment not a cost – if they are the right people. A cost is what you get when you hire the wrong people.

If you must have a 'warm body' immediately, always hire a "temp." They are skilled, useful and not on your payroll as an employee. Use their talents until you can 'hire right.'

Nothing replaces the excellent selection of people.

H
HIRING

Good Managers Hire The Best People. Poor Managers Hire The Worst People.

You Can Tell the Quality of the Leader by the People Around Her/Him.

An efficient leader always surrounds himself/herself with excellent people. A weak leader always surrounds himself/herself with less capable people.

An effective leader is secure in his/her ability and future success. He/she will focus on generating opportunities for organizational growth and profit.

A weak leader is insecure. He/she will focus on solving problems and protecting his/her 'kingdom' rather than on growing the business.

A leader's job is to grow the business – to create opportunity. It is not to maintain the status quo. We can train "monkeys" to do that.

Average leaders are 'maintainers.'

Good leaders are 'growers.'

Great leaders are "grower/developers."

We cannot have 'maintainers' in today's competitive global marketplace. They drain our resources and limit our growth.

Hire and develop the best people into the best leaders. They will grow your business and your organization.

> ### FARANDA MAXIM
>
> *Poor Hiring
> Is The Main Cause For
> Firing*

Hiring Right Makes Money. Hiring Wrong Costs Money.

Hiring right will save you hours of time and a great deal of cost and pain. Hiring wrong is expensive.

The average cost of replacing a secretary is between $7,000 and $10,000. Poor hiring causes firing.

Hiring the right person for the right job is a science and an art. Matching the right person to the right job on a continuous basis is one secret to successful growth and profit.

Firing is an essential part of effective management and leadership. It can also be an expensive admission that your hiring practices are not well conceived and administered.

Hiring right adds to your bottom line. Hiring wrong subtracts from your bottom line.

Concentrate on hiring the right people the first time.

H

HELL

FARANDA MAXIM

Hell Is Seeing the Person We Never Wanted to Be In the Mirror

Sometimes in Life and in Business Looking in the Mirror is 'Hell'.

The best leaders always take the time to review what they have done, what they are doing and how they are doing it. They are not afraid of looking in the mirror.

The best leaders look in the mirror every day to see if the person they see is the person they want to be. When this is not so, they make the appropriate changes.

Every leader's life is based on a series of choices that are made on a daily basis.

Even very successful leaders make poor choices at times. However, they correct poor choices quickly. Their batting average of good to poor choices is always quite favorable.

Life is choices. Look in the mirror to see if you like yours.

> **FARANDA MAXIM**
>
> *To be "Intelligent"*
> *You must*
> *Adapt to change*

Leaders Who Survive and Prosper Have Learned to Adapt to Change.

The medical definition of intelligence is "the ability to adapt to change."

The standard definition of intelligence is "the inherent ability to learn."

All of us know people who have great "inherent ability" to learn but who have achieved little or nothing. They go through life with great intelligence and little accomplishment.

What good is ability if it never becomes accomplishment?

Give me adaptability any day. If you can learn to adapt to the changing world around you, you can survive and prosper.

Intelligence without adaptability is as useless as a chicken without an egg. The chicken will sit around all day clucking over everything and accomplishing nothing.

Give me the egg. It won't make any noise, and at least, I can eat it.

I

IMAGE

Help A Person To Develop An Image... He/She Will Live Up To It!

A Positive Self-Image Increases a Person's Value and Accomplishment.

Some of the best people have the worst image.

They are devalued because of their perceived value rather than their actual value.

Some of the worst people have the best image.

They are valued because of their perceived value rather than their actual value.

A person's perception by others is different from a person's perception of themselves.

Successful people do not allow other people's perceptions to devalue or undermine them. They simply continue on their path to success, secure in their own ability and value.

An effective leader helps others to develop a successful image based on competence and strong self-esteem. Once people develop a positive self-image, they will live up to it.

Helping people develop a positive self-image is like opening a window on a warm and sunny spring day. The air overwhelms you with possibilities!

FARANDA MAXIM

To Improve Your Image…
Find Out What People
Know and Remember
About You.

Image is Not an Accident Unless You Allow It to be.

We always assume market research is for securing critical information on products and services of large corporations.

Marketing research tools are also effective for securing critical information on our own image as perceived by others.

Each of us has several images. We have an image to ourself. We have an image to our family. We have an image to our boss. We have an image to our friends. We have an image to our customers.

Few people have a uniform image to everyone.

If you want to establish an honest and effective image of yourself to your different 'audiences,' you must work on it. To work on it you must first know what others think of you. Ask questions. Use psychological profiles and 'imaging' forms. Listen, then act.

Your image and reputation are your most valuable assets.

To improve your image you must first value it. Treat it as you would a bar of gold in your safe deposit box – safeguard it, insure it, enjoy it and build on it.

An image is not an accident unless you allow it to be.

I

INNOVATION

Innovation Is A New Way
To Do An Old Thing
Or
An Old Way To Do
A New Thing

Be an Effective Innovator and You Will Get Job Offers Every Month.

Invention and innovation are not the same thing.

Invention is the process of assembling new elements into a marketable product or service or technology or idea.

Innovation is the process of re-assembling existing elements into a new version of an existing product or service or technology or idea.

Successful leaders learn to be inventive and innovative. Since few leaders have the true capacity to be inventive, most focus on innovation.

Innovation is often based on discovery.

Discovery is the process of looking at the same thing as everyone else and thinking something different.

Innovation is based on creative imagination.

Imagination must be rewarded if it is to continue.

> "The amount a person uses his/her imagination is inversely proportional to the amount of punishment he/she receives for using it."
>
> T. W. Faranda

Learn to be innovative and you will get job offers every month.

> **FARANDA MAXIM**
>
> *What You Do __TO__ or __FOR__ A Person Is The Difference Between Productivity and "Problemtivity."*

McDonalds Says, "We Do It All For You!"

McDonalds Corporation is the most successful franchise operation in the world. It is also one of the most successful corporations of any type in the world.

Their entire customer satisfaction policy revolves around the phrase, "We do it all for you!" Just think how their image would change if their slogan was changed to ... "We do it all to you!"

This would alter the entire meaning of their communication and would negatively affect their leadership image.

What you do to or for a person does make a difference. People respond with quality performance and high productivity when they know you care about them personally. That's what doing things for people can create.

People always know when you are doing things *to* them.

People respond to this by delivering "problemtivity." There will be an increase in tardiness, long breaks and absenteeism. There will be a decrease in quality, volume, productivity and profitability. There will be a significant decrease in customer satisfaction. This will guarantee your organization's decline.

Leaders do things for their people. Foremen should be there with their people on the line. Supervisors should serve coffee to their secretaries. Management should serve supervisors and workers. Everyone should serve the customer.

Service starts *inside* an organization as well as *outside.*

L

LEADERSHIP

FARANDA MAXIM

Leadership Is An Art. Without Drama The Play Closes

A Good Leader Always Knows His/Her Part. A Good Leader Always Plays It.

Leaders must take positive, successful and strong action, combined with drama, to demonstrate leadership.

Drama is the catalyst to keep the play alive.

Drama should never enter into the reason for the decision or action, but it should always color the successful end result.

Victor Kiam uses drama to demonstrate his shavers.

Steven Jobs uses drama to demonstrate his computer.

Lee Iacocca uses drama to demonstrate his cars.

Successful leaders know how to utilize drama as part of the methodology of effective and exciting leadership.

Boring leadership – leadership without drama – will close down even a good play.

Learn to be a player. Learn your part and play it.

Without drama the play closes.

> FARANDA MAXIM
>
> *A Leader's Role Is To*
> *Serve The People…*
> *Not To Be Served.*

The World's Great Religious Books All Agree that the Leader's Role is to Serve the People.

We are now in a society that values *being* served rather than serving. We are now in a society where leaders expect to be royalty rather than servants.

All great leaders have the ability to be treated as royalty while serving the people – to ask for nothing and be given everything. The people give them this willingly and openly as long as the leader serves the people. Once the leader starts serving himself/herself rather than the people, the people withdraw their favors.

A leader can fool people only for a given period of time. Eventually, their motives and reputation catch up to them.

Learn to serve people.

Do not ask your secretary to get you coffee. Ask if you can get him/her coffee.

Do not ask someone else to volunteer for a task force until you have served on a task force.

Leaders who learn to serve the people are served in return.

L

LEADERSHIP

People Are More Convinced By The Depth Of Your Belief Than by The Power of Your Argument.

Successful Leadership Must be Based on a Firm and Ethical Set of Beliefs.

Conviction. Ethics. Values. Beliefs. These are the words that have an impact on people. These are the words that succeed in moving people to action.

People always know when a leader really believes in something. They sense conviction. They observe that you truly *live* your values and beliefs.

Anyone can sprout beliefs with conviction. The secret is whether you *live* your beliefs. The proof is what you do and not what you say you do.

All the great leaders of the world have lived their beliefs.

You cannot argue with conviction unless you have depth of belief. You can argue with power. People will always know the difference and act accordingly.

Many "empty" people have argued with power and some have even been successful. It is an empty feeling to argue with power for something you do not believe in. It is a joy to argue with conviction for that in which you believe.

Make your choice – an "empty" person or a full one.

What you do today does make a difference.

Live what you believe. Start today. Don't let an "empty" person argue you into emptiness. Stay full.

FARANDA MAXIM

A Good Leader Knows How To Get Out Of Trouble A Great Leader Knows How To Avoid It

---

Preventive Leadership is Better than Crisis Leadership.

Too many managers and leaders have sleepless afternoons because they live in a world of constant "crisis management."

Crisis management eliminates all hopes of fulfilling your destiny as a successful leader/manager. You will spend your life as a dog chasing its tail – always going in circles, never going forward to achieve something significant.

Preventive leadership makes things happen or stops things from happening. This is a pro-active position of strength and not a reactive position of weakness.

A pro-active position allows you to stay out of trouble rather than spending all of your time getting out of trouble.

Peter Drucker, the world's most famous writer on management and leadership, wrote a simple but very powerful statement.

> "Your job as a manager is not just to solve problems.
> Your job is to create opportunities for your organization."

This is the best pro-active leader advice known.

Getting out of trouble is a good skill. Avoiding trouble is a great skill. Great leaders avoid trouble.

L

LEADERSHIP

> *Questions*
> *are a greater source of*
> *knowledge than answers.*
> *Learn to ask great*
> *Questions*

Ask Good Questions, Shut Up and Listen. (This is a Modern Version of Socrates' Philosophy)

"A good leader can be identified by the quality of his/her questions, rather than by the quality of his/her answers."   (Socrates)

A good question shows that you have enough knowledge of the subject at hand to know what you need to know.

Formulating and asking a good question is an art form. Master it and you master the art of securing critical information and helping others feel part of the team.

Most good leaders master the art of answering questions. Only the great leaders master the art of asking them.

A good question will give you power without looking for it. A good question will generate more ideas from others than any other method of feedback. A good question will show others your strengths.

Socrates knew what he was talking about. Listen to him.

> FARANDA MAXIM
>
> *Leadership Is...*
> *Motivating...*
> *not manipulating;*
> *Listening...*
> *not talking;*
> *Nurturing...*
> *not persuading.*

You Can Choose Your Own Leadership and Management Style.

There are no "tricks" to leadership and management. There are only proven techniques that work with people.

Communication works. Motivation works. Listening works. Nurturing works. Kindness works. Sincerity works. Caring works.

People's lives are more complicated today than ever before in history. People themselves are not.

We have known for hundred of years what motivates people. We have known what qualities of leadership impress people. We have known what people want in order for them to be involved and productive and happy.

Our job as a leader is to give it to them.

Develop three to five leadership styles that work with each person as an individual. Use different styles for different people, different situations, different environments. This is called situational leadership.

Remember, a leader cannot motivate groups. He/she can only motivate individuals within groups. When all the individuals are motivated you get quality, productivity, profitability and growth.

L

LEADERSHIP

*Strong Leaders
Always Hire People
Who Are Better
Than They Are
Weak Leaders
Always Hire People
Who Are Worse
Than They Are*

You *Can* Tell the Quality of a Leader by the People He/She Has Around Them.

Weak and insecure leaders place people around them who make them comfortable. They like people who see things in the same manner as they do, who "think" like them.

Remember the old quotation:

> "When two people agree all the time, one of them is unnecessary."
>
> (Author Unknown)

Strong leaders place people around them who can get the job done in a positive and productive mannner. They like people who see things in a different manner than they do, who do not "think" like them.

Strong leaders like diversity of thought. They like new ideas, new perspectives, new methods.

A weak leader will always "lead" a group that is standing still or going backwards. They actually think that maintaining their market share, profitability and sales volume is progress. It is not – it is stagnation.

A strong leader will always lead a group that is moving forward. This is the essence of leadership.

> **FARANDA MAXIM**
>
> *Weak Leaders*
> *Keep Control*
> *Strong Leaders*
> *Give It Away*

Control is a Weak and Insecure Leader's Excuse for Power.

All leaders need to utilize effective control mechanisms such as quality control standards, production quotas, budgets and reports.

These are methods of maintaining control of the functional business.

Strong leaders get control by giving it away.

They selectively choose people who can handle power and authority to achieve a specific set of goals and objectives. They set the goals and objectives together in order to insure that they strategically support the organization's mission.

Control is only as good as the leader establishing the system. Good leaders gain more control by reducing the controls to a few well-designed and effective systems.

A strong leader makes sure that everyone at all levels of the organization understands the control systems and can use them.

A strong leader makes sure that there are fewer management levels so the controls are more effective and timely.

Start giving away your control so you will get stronger.

L

LEADERSHIP

> *A Weak Leader*
> *Takes Credit*
> *A Strong Leader*
> *Gives It Away*

Credit is Useless If You Can't Pay the Bill.

Giving people credit is one of the most effective and least expensive methods of effectively motivating them.

Strong leaders do not need to steal the credit for other people's ideas. They gain strength by crediting others. They generate additional ideas by utilizing the mental resources of others.

Weak leaders think they need to take the credit for all good ideas because "it was under their leadership that the ideas were developed."

People hate credit stealers.

It takes a mature and successful person to understand that power comes from creating opportunities and from growing the organization.

Positive power is a function of developing an effective team. An effective team is a combination of many effective individuals who have learned to work toward the same goals.

When you give credit away, the individuals and the team respond with greater productivity.

Giving credit away to others is the greatest gift you can ever give yourself. When you give credit away, it comes back to you threefold.

> ### FARANDA MAXIM
> ## *Creating Opportunities*
> ## *Makes Money*
> ## *Solving Problems*
> ## *Spends Money*

You Must Generate More Than You Spend To Remain Profitable.

No one can succeed in business by solving problems. Problems are in themselves an indication of what is wrong with the system or the product or the service.

Solving problems costs money. Money should be used primarily for creating opportunities and not for solving problems. Creating opportunities generates new money for the organization and fosters growth.

There is an exception.

Spend any amount of money necessary to solve your customer's problems and provide total customer satisfaction.

Your customers are your business. Without them you will not need to solve problems – you will have neither problems nor business.

Focus on solving problems by eliminating the causes of the problems.

Solve quality problems by establishing an effective quality program that everyone understands and believes in. Solve production, finance, marketing and other functional problems the same way.

Use your money to create opportunities not just to solve problems.

L
LEADERSHIP

Leadership Is Person Specific
An Effective Leader Needs
Different Leadership Styles
To Be Effective
With Different People

One Car Usually Does Not Meet a Family's Total Needs!

To be an effective leader you need three to five different leadership styles.

The different styles need to be applied to different people or sometimes, to the same person at different times. They need to be applied to different circumstances, industries and situations as they occur.

A leader with only one style is just as handicapped as a one-car family with a stationwagon. The stationwagon may serve a great purpose for some uses, but it definitely does not fit the bill for a formal night out.

The best leaders use their repertoire of styles as a conductor uses different instruments in the orchestra. Each instrument has a definite purpose. The conductor's job is to see that the purpose is fulfilled for the greatest impact on the audience. The conductor seeks harmony.

Great leaders also seek harmony. They build individuals into effective teams to fulfill the mission of the organization. They see to it that each person fulfills his/her own goals while the organization fulfills its goals.

The great leaders know that leadership is "person specific." They spend time with their people as an investment in the organization's future. They care about their people and they demonstrate it.

A "person-specific" leader knows his/her people so well that he/she can give them what they need, when they need it. This creates loyalty and commitment for the leader.

> # *Lead All People As Volunteers And Not Employees*

L
LEADERSHIP

We Treat Volunteers Better Than Employees Because Volunteers Do Not Have to Return.

Volunteer labor is one of the great benefits to many organizations. Yet few leaders know how to harness the power of volunteers.

Volunteers do not always work for the same reasons as employees. They may not need the income. They may not need the job at all. They may simply enjoy the accomplishments of work and the companionship of their colleagues.

Most leaders treat volunteers better than employees. They say "hello" and "thank you" and many other motivating words.

If all leaders would use these same motivating words for their employees, those same employees would be more productive. Entire attitudes would improve. Quality would improve. Productivity would improve. There might actually be a positive productivity revolution.

This is not expensive.

This is not hard to learn.

Do It.

L
LIFE

Life Is The Only Capital
A Human Being Has...
The Rest is
All Loose Change

"Wisdom is Knowing What to Do Next. Virtue is Doing It."
David Jordan

Life is a "beach" or a "bitch" depending on what t-shirt you are looking at and what you personally believe in.

But life *is* life. You can live it and do all of the things that you have always wanted to do. Or, you can simply exist and do nothing.

You are not worth very much from a physical point of view. A prime T-Bone is worth more on the market than the total worth of your body on the market. You body exists to fulfill the desires of your mind and soul.

To live life means to use your mental, emotional, physical and spiritual capital to the fullest. It means casting off all the negatives that weigh you down. It means choosing your friends so you only spend time with people who are "nutritious" for you.

It means throwing away all of the uselessness of life that comes from an overabundance of physical possessions and a lack of spiritual possessions.

Dying is a good way to understand this concept.

Some people get too close to death and then get a second chance to live. They always seem to change their life when they live it the "second" time. They do a better job of it.

There is a lesson to be learned from this.

FARANDA MAXIM

Life Is An Unfinished Symphony... But You Write The Score!

Choices Make Your Life...But You Make the Choices.

Living makes much more sense than existing.

Existing is a passive waste of time and brainpower. It exhausts your mind, body and spirit. You never have any energy. You never find yourself interested in anything or anyone other than yourself.

Existing is self-indulgence and selfishness.

Living is much harder than existing.

It requires you to be part of the world. It causes you to renew your mind, body and spirit. You have more energy as a rule although at times you are joyfully exhausted. You find yourself more interested in others and less interested in yourself. Time doesn't just pass – it flies.

Life is full of experiences, some good and some painful. The good ones help you recover from the painful ones. The painful ones help you grow to enjoy more of the good ones.

Living is harder, but it is definitely better. You have the choice. To live or to exist.

A symphony has many movements. Each movement is written in the score. If you don't like the movement, re-write the score.

Life is an unfinished symphony. So are you.

Get busy and live.

L
LISTENING

*We Do Not Need
To Teach People
To Think...
We Need To
Allow People To Think...
And Listen When They Do*

Listening is a Positive Leadership Act.

"A wise old owl sat in an oak, the more he saw the less he spoke, the less he spoke the more he heard, why can't we be like that wise old bird?"

(Author Unkown)

Listening is one of the most highly rated skills when rating a leader. The better the listener, the higher the rating. Why do we talk more than listen?

Our society values talking more than listening. We get rewarded for talking. We do not get rewarded for listening. It all starts in our childhood. Unfortunately, it continues in our adulthood.

People know how to think. Let them. Then listen to them. They will amaze you with their ability if you let them.

Other cultures value listening more than talking. Their economies are growing at a very fast pace. Perhaps we can learn something from these other cultures who are so much older than ours.

Practice listening to others. It is a skill. You must practice it to get better at it.

Listening is no different than golf. The typical golf pro hits a chip shot in practice more than one hundred times before hitting it in competition. That allows the chip shot to work when he/she really needs it.

Practice your chip shot so it works when you need it.

FARANDA MAXIM

*The Leader Who Listens
May Have More To Say...
Than The Leader
Who Talks*

The Listening Leader/Manager Sends Positive "Value Messages" to Others.

From birth we get excited when someone listens to us. The closer the someone is to us, the more we get excited.

A boss/worker relationship can be a close relationship if for no other reason than the amount of time involved. Most people spend more time at work than at home. Most people see their boss as much as they see their spouse.

One way to show people that you really care about them is to listen to them.

One way to make more money for your organization is to listen to them.

One way to build a quality team that works is to listen to them.

Many people talk a great deal but have little to say. Leaders who listen well usually talk a little less but have a great deal more to say.

Leaders who listen usually get listened to.

Hum ...

M

MANAGEMENT

Poor Management:
On The Surface
Very Little
Is Happening
Beneath The Surface
Nothing Is Happening!

Poor Management is an Insidious Epidemic – We Need a New Vaccine to Wipe It Out!

Poor management is management that doesn't deliver results based on the organization's goals. It is management that fails to focus on the mission of the organization. It is management that develops a "laissez faire" attitude of passive contentment.

Good management is active management. It focuses all of management's resources toward the organization's mission. It redefines its goals and objectives.

We still have management teams who feel that maintaining the organization means success.

Sears is an example of this posture. Sears has recently tried to sell its "home" – the Sears Tower in Chicago. That shows you the impact of a maintenance management (no growth) culture.

Wal-Mart, with over 1100 stores and only three management levels, is an example of a growth management culture. They are opening three stores every month and beating Sears in every business category.

When it *appears* that nothing is happening, nothing usually is happening. This is not "management."

If the surface is smooth, there had better be bubbles on the way up.

FARANDA MAXIM

Crisis Management Has Caused Many Managers Golfless Afternoons

You Can't Take Time to Play Golf When You Live in a World of Constant Crisis.

The best managers always have time to plan for the future. They build in planning time. They also have time to play golf.

Good financial consultants tell us that the people who save the most money are those who put away money at the start of the month – before spending it. No one can save money with an attitude of saving what is left at the end of the month.

This is true of planning time. You must put the time aside at the start of the month – before you "spend it." Time is money. Look at it that way.

All of us may face periods of crisis management. Make sure the period doesn't become a sentence, or even worse, a paragraph.

Crisis management has never been a successful management strategy in the past.

Don't make a habit of it.

M
MANAGEMENT

Management is Active. Administration is Passive. Success Lives in an Active World.

A manager acts to make something happen or not happen.

An administrator waits for something to happen and then rushes to consult the policy manual to determine what to do.

Fire all administrators.

The world belongs to those who are ahead of it, not to those who are behind it.

Managers are ahead of it. Administrators are not.

Fire all administrators.

M
MARKETS

> **FARANDA MAXIM**
>
> *Separate "Suspects"*
> *From "Prospects."*
> *"Prospects"*
> *Are Willing And Able*
> *To Buy.*

A Prospect is an Investment.
A Suspect is a Cost.

The most successful organizations and leaders learn to focus on a narrow band (or several narrow bands) of potential customers who fit a pre-established criteria. This is a target market or a market niche.

Even the larger firms such as 3M, IBM and others do not scatter their sales and marketing effort over a wide spectrum. This is inefficient, expensive and foolish. Instead, they focus their resources to reach a specific target market of customers who are able and willing to buy their products or services.

Successful organizations do market research to determine their target markets. Market research is what defines the narrow bands on which to focus. Market research is a combination of demographic information, market needs, market potential, product/service capacity, psychographic information, sociographic information and other factors.

Organizations use market research because it works.

Use market research to define your specific target markets. Then separate "suspects" from "prospects." Go after prospects only. You will make more profit by serving more customers. This really does work.

M
MINDSET

FARANDA MAXIM

Change Your Thinking Change Your Life.

Your Mindset is Your Choice.
Your Mindset is Your Life.

There are some things in our life and our career that we can choose. Mindset is one of them.

We can choose to be a winner or a loser.

We can choose to grow or to shrivel up.

We can choose to choose ...

Choose well.

Your mindset determines your state of being.

> "The greatest revolution ... is the discovery that human beings, by changing the inner attitudes of their minds, can change the outer aspects of their lives."
>
> William James

Choose well. You only have one life to choose. You live your choices.

You cannot blame anyone else for your choices. You made them.

Take responsibility for your choices and your life.

Then your life will really start to be worth something.

Market Share is One True Measure of Business Success.

When organizations are being managed effectively, they are increasing their market share.

Many leaders think they have increased their market share when in fact the market has simply gotten bigger. They have more revenue but they do not have more market share.

They have not done well. They have been lucky.

A good leader increases market share in an increasing market.

A great leader increases market share in both an increasing and decreasing market.

This is excellence of performance rather than luck.

Market share represents profitable growth. Profitable growth represents a future.

When a market is shrinking, someone will always be buying up the losers and/or stealing their market share. In a decreasing market, someone will always be doing better.

Make sure that "someone" is you!

O
OUTPLACEMENT

An Effective Leader Outplaces Poor Performers To The Competition

You Cannot Keep Poor Performers and Expect to Succeed.

The first job of an effective leader is to identify the performance levels of his/her people.

The second job is to attempt to correct poor performance.

The third job is to fire all poor performers who do not correct their work.

The fourth is to outplace poor performers to your competition.

If you "outplace" your poor performers, you will send a performance expectation signal to your people. Marginal performers will either improve, quit or expect to be fired. This will help the performance and productivity of the organization.

If you outplace your poor performers, you will have time to recognize and reward your top performers for their achievements. Top performers need to be recognized and rewarded if you want them to continue to be top performers.

If you outplace your poor performers you will have more time to plan and create since you will have fewer problems to solve.

"Outplacement" is a lovely word, but an even more lovely deed.

> **FARANDA MAXIM**
>
> *You Can't Buy*
> *A Good Plan*
> *At A Wholesale Price.*
> *Pay Retail*
> *And*
> *Buy Commitment.*

A Great Plan is Useless Unless Everyone Buys Into It.

A plan should be simple enough for the lowest level person to understand it.

A plan should be logical enough for the lowest level person to accept it.

A plan should be flexible enough for the lowest level person to use it.

If you try to cheat on the planning process by using a "wholesale" mindset you will get a wholesale result.

Pay "retail" for your plan. Spend the money you need on market research, talent and resources to create a plan at "retail."

A retail plan works if it sets a tone for the entire organization. A plan that works buys commitment from everyone.

A plan that is workable allows people to buy into it. What people buy into works.

P

PLANNING

Plan What You Plan to Do.
Plan What You Plan to Teach.

No successful leader makes a bank presentation, a sales presentation, a manufacturing presentation or any other presentation without a plan.

Don't go in empty handed.

Visualize your ideas. Use charts, pictures, graphs, diagrams, models, prototypes or any vehicle necessary to visualize your main ideas.

Many weak proposals have succeeded through strong visual presentation. Many strong proposals have failed through weak visual representation.

Preparation is the key to presentation.

Don't go in empty headed.

Always have a plan A, B and C prepared ahead of time. If plan A isn't working, bridge to plan B and even to plan C if necessary.

Always be prepared to change your presentation based on how well it is working.

An effective presentation is a presentation that works.

*The Correct Time
To Get Information
Is <u>Before</u> You Need It.*

P
POWER

Getting Information "Late" Reduces Its Strategic Value.

Information is power. The timing of information is power. The use of information is power.

Information power decreases with age.

You need information before you need it. Having information before you need it allows you to plan the timing or use of the information.

Fortunes have been made and lost based on the power of information.

In ancient days, the China traders developed several methods of gathering information on availability and pricing of goods desired for shipment in and out of China. Flag signals, for example, were developed for ships sailing within sight of a Chinese harbor. The flag signals told those on shore what cargo was on board and what the market price was for outbound goods. This strategic information allowed those on land to sell or buy with advance information and make powerful and profitable deals.

The information was needed when the ship landed. But the information was much more powerful in advance.

Those who had the most advance information made fortunes. Those who did not, lost them.

Information is power. Learn to use it. Learn to collect it before you need it.

P

POWER

There Are Three Stages Of Power:
1. Telling Others What To Do.
2. Telling Others What You Want Done.
3. Asking Others To Help You Do It.
Positive Power People Only Use The Third Stage.

Positive Power is Related to Negative Power as the Mongoose is to the Snake.

A mongoose is a friendly and personable animal that is often kept as a pet in India.

A mongoose, however, hates snakes. When a snake appears a mongoose becomes an instant death machine to the snake. If the snake senses a mongoose's presence, it does not appear.

Positive power is the art of successfully asking people to help you. Negative power is the macho act of demanding tribute.

Negative power does not appear when it senses positive power. Like the snake, it knows better.

Truly powerful people are for the most part, positive power people. For every J. R. Ewing, there are ten Ross Perot's.

Learn how to use positive power to strengthen your professional career and personal relationships.

This is not a strategy or a technique. It is a way of living and leading.

Lead with positive power and people will continue to let you lead.

> FARANDA MAXIM
>
> *In Any Partnership*
> *Every Partner Will*
> *Think His/Her Project*
> *Is The Most Important.*

A Partnership is a Marriage of Un-Equals.

No partnership has ever been created equal.

Someone always has the upper hand, the controlling vote, the overriding influence. This is seldom acknowledged and often unspoken. But it is real.

The only partnerships that work over time are those that are structured and have common goals, ambitions, visions and values. These should be in writing.

A partnership is the hardest form of organization to manage and lead successfully.

A designated "managing partner" should be responsible for overall mission, strategy, growth and leadership. The other partners should agree to let the managing partner do his/her job – in writing. This is seldom done. This is why partnerships are the hardest organizations to manage.

Except in smaller partnerships, the managing partner should not be responsible for "billable hours," weekly work quotas" or any other performance measurement that other partners must operate under. Their role is leadership – the coordination of resources to generate growth and profit of the organization.

Partnerships are not equal. The managing partner is there to maintain the balance of power so that all partners benefit and the organization grows.

FARANDA MAXIM

When Everyone Goes East... Go West

Find Out What Your Competition is Doing. Do Not Do It.

Ticketmaster Corporation established a mission to take over control of their industry from Ticketron, the firmly established market leader. They have succeeded.

Ticketmaster's strategy was to find out what Ticketron was doing. They then organized a new and better system and combined it with fast, efficient, personalized service to the customer.

Ticketron become fatter. Ticketmaster stayed lean. Ticketron become technologically obsolescent. Ticketmaster become technologically the leader. Ticketron got impersonal. Ticketmaster got personal. Ticketron lost. Ticketmaster won.

It works.

Do nothing until you discover what your competition is doing. Then, do not do it. Be an original, not a copy.

Learn to do it faster and better. Learn to care about your customer. It works because so few of us are doing it.

> ## *If You Can Do Without Profit You Are Probably Not Helping Anyone.*

P
PROFIT

Profit is the World's "Mover and Shaker."

Profit is healthy, greed is not.

Profit is the momentum that keeps us capitalists, not communists. Communism does not work. China and Russia are finally learning this lesson and they are changing!

When there is no "mover or shaker," there is "tradition."

Tradition at its best is stability. Tradition at its worst is stagnation.

Tradition has depth. But tradition has no meaning without growth.

Profit is a tradition in America. If you want to help the world, push profit. Only profitable organizations seem to contribute to world causes and world peace. Communists never seem to be able to feed their own people let alone help others. America helps the world.

Profit helps everyone.

P

PROFIT

Cost Centers become Profit Centers When they contribute to total customer satisfaction

Read Peter Drucker. He is the Master. Learn From Him. There are No Profit Centers Within the Business. There are Only Cost Centers.

Spending resources is only effective if it leads to growth and profitability. Growth and profitability is the test of what is an investment versus what is a cost.

To incur cost without a plan of how to turn it into an investment is leadership negligence. To incur long term costs without turning them into investments is leadership criminality.

A cost center only serves a useful purpose if it makes it possible for the organization to generate additional resource opportunities. If it does not meet this criteria, remove it.

Cost centers can be useful if they focus on the goal of customer satisfaction. If they assist the organization in winning, retaining and satisfying its customers, they are an investment not a cost.

Managers focus on opportunity. Administrators focus on problems. Leaders focus on growth and profitability.

Read Peter Drucker. He has been saying it clearly for over 30 years.

1. *The Best of Peter Drucker* by Peter Drucker. (Harper & Row, 1977)

2. *Innovation and Entrepreneurship* by Peter Drucker. (Harper & Row, 1985)

> *The Polaroid Mentality Always Provides A Fuzzy Picture.*

Q
QUICKFIXES

There are No Quickfixes.

We live in a world today where everyone wants and expects instant solutions to complex problems. There are none.

A Polaroid mentality shows that quickfix thinking is a useless exercise in frustration.

The only true solutions are those that enhance the long and short term use of resources in a strategic manner.

There is a substantial difference between a quickfix and a solution.

A quickfix plugs the hole in the dike.

A solution repairs the damage. A solution is long-term philosophy. There is often pain in the short-term when you have an effective long-term solution.

Effective leaders do not indulge themselves in a "Polaroid quickfix mentality." They want pictures that will look as good in 2089 as well as in 1989.

Go for a solution and get a clear picture.

Q
QUALITY

Management Cannot Mandate Quality. The Quality Concept Works When Everyone in the Organization Buys Into the Concept.

Quality is a piece of the customer satisfaction puzzle. All pieces of the puzzle must be in place if an organization is to generate customer satisfaction.

Customer satisfaction is the main variable of long term growth and profitability.

Quality is expensive in the short term and cheap in the long term. Ask Japan. Forty years ago "Made in Japan" meant junk. Today, "Made in Japan" means quality. Japan is doing very well today.

Everyone in the organization must believe in quality. The people at the bottom are more important than those at the top in regard to quality.

Quality is not just an "issue," it is a critical piece of the customer satisfaction puzzle.

Without quality the puzzle will never be solved.

FARANDA MAXIM

Give All Credit Away
Accept All Blame

Credit Bonds People to You.

People despise leaders who take credit for their ideas.

People respect leaders who give them credit for their ideas.

Even if you take a good but unworkable idea and change it to workable idea, give all credit to the person who created the idea. You will build respect and credibility with your people.

Those you give credit to will return credit to you. You will have a constant stream of "third party testimonials" to your strengths as a leader.

Recognition is one of the most powerful human motivators. It costs nothing but generates immeasurable good will and productivity.

People want to be recognized as part of the "team." They want to be recognized as individuals and not as "cogs" in a machine.

Use recognition as a vehicle for success.

Successful leaders recognize and credit other people.

R
RESULTS

Accomplishments Not Activities Lead To Success.

Being "Busy" Never Made a Person Successful.

Our society tends to associate being busy with being productive. There is no correlation between them.

Accomplishments are tangible, and productive. They lead to results.

Always reward results. Remember the axiom. "We do that for which we are rewarded."

Results are measurable. "Being busy" is not.

There is a correlation between people who are simply "busy" and people who generate few results. Being "busy" without generating results is a cover up for those who cannot face the fact of their incompetence.

It is more effective to complete one critical project than to be busy on ten projects.

An unfinished project is a liability – a cost. A finished project is an asset – an investment.

Don't be "busy." Be productive. Get results.

A leader looks for accomplishments and not activities.

> It is not enough to be busy. The question is "What are we busy about?"
>
> Thoreau

FARANDA MAXIM

"The Camel's Back Syndrome"...
It's Not The Big Things
That Help You Keep
Your Customer.
It's The Little Things.

The Weight of Four Thousand Rose Petals...Will Break a Camel's Back.

Your customers do not stop doing business with you due to a big error or problem. Your customers stop doing business with you when the collective weight of all the "little things" is greater than your value to them.

Customers do remember all the "little things" you do to or for them. Especially when something goes wrong.

They do remember the extra time you spent with them when they needed it. They do remember the special delivery service you provided when they ran short of parts. They do remember the thank you notes, the relationship building lunches, the training sessions for their people. They do remember.

In most cases it is not price, or terms, or product, or service alone that bonds customers to you. It is the little things you do for your customers.

The strength of a relationship – marital or professional – is built on bonding. Bonding is built on the "little things."

It's the little things that help you keep your customers.

R
RELATIONSHIPS

Never Close A Door Without Opening A Window!

Always Open a Window of Hope if You Expect to See a Ray of Sunshine.

One very effective way of demonstrating that you will not accept poor or mediocre performance is to refuse to give someone a scheduled raise.

One very effective way to destroy any hope of getting improvement from that person is to close the door and not open a window.

How many of us would be motivated to improve if we knew it would be one year before another performance review would take place?

Always open a window ...

Schedule another performance review for three months ahead. Tell the person what they must do within the three months to get their raise. Meet with them every month to make sure they are doing it. They will surprise you with their success.

(So will everyone else when they realize that you mean business ... and that you are fair!)

Relationships are the key to productivity, performance and profitable long term growth.

Develop them, respect them, keep opening windows.

FARANDA MAXIM

Too Many Organizations Today are Capital Based. Be People Based.

Successful Organizations Focus on the Success of Their People So That Their People Will Focus on the Success of Their Organization.

Organizations that focus on customer satisfaction as a mission have learned to be people based.

Only your people can provide true long term customer satisfaction and gain the customer bonding that guarantees growth and profitability. For your people to be successful in this customer bonding process they must be trained. Training is a central commitment by people based organizations.

All the capital in the world will not replace trained people.

A $5 million advertising campaign to generate potential customer leads is useless if the people handling the leads turn off the potential customers when they call or come in.

A $5 million quality program is useless without the training and commitment of all employees at all levels in the organization.

People based organizations treat training and training executives as an integral part of the organization. They put their best people in training situations, they fund the training function at a level greater than the industry average.

Be a people based organization and help your people help you.

R

RULES

Today...
The Only Rule Is That
There Are No Rules.

In a World of Constant and Aggressive Change, Rules Can Be Limiting. The Fewer Rules You Have, the Faster You Can Innovate and Change to Beat Your Competitor.

Organizations that have too many rules, or rules that are too inflexible, will stifle creativity and innovation.

Rules need to be broad brush strokes – outlines of suggested patterns, not pencil thin inflexible lines.

Leaders must be given the opportunity to operate within these broad brush strokes. They must be able to bend and twist "rules," to fit the situation at hand. You cannot tie leaders with rules and expect them to be flexible. Free them. Empower them. They will surprise you.

> "Never tell a man how to do something. Tell him what to do and let him decide how to do it. He will surprise you with his ingenuity."
>
> (General Patton)

There are no rules today – except those you make up as you need them. Stay loose. Be flexible.

The key to tomorrow's success is innovation and change – breaking a trail rather than following a path.

Learn to bend instead of break and you will stay ahead of your competition.

*Success Has Walls
But No Barriers.*

Success is Not Open-Ended.

"Success" is one of the most difficult words to define. It is a "person" specific word. Everyone has their own definition of success relative to their specific life at a specific moment of time.

> "What matters is not the meaning of life in general, but the specific meaning of a person's life at a given moment."
> (Viktor Frankil)

Success in life changes at different stages of life. It is never open-ended. It is definable within a specific stage of life. Success is based on personal values. If you achieve what you value at a specific moment in time, you are a "success" based on your own personal definition.

The opposite of success is not failure to achieve. It is failure to try. When you fail to try you cannot expect to succeed. When you try and fail, you can still try again.

If a goal is incorrect for you, then failure to achieve is not failure. Failure is not trying to achieve it. Failure is not recognizing that you are aiming at the wrong target. Success is changing the target and then trying to hit it. Success is achieving it.

Success is built on walls. The walls are moveable, not fixed. Success has walls but no barriers.

S

SUCCESS

There Can be No Success Without Standards

Success Must be Defined and Measured to be Achieved.

We do that for which we are rewarded. We are rewarded for that which we achieve – if we know we have achieved it.

Without standards to define what we have achieved, there is no achievement. We cannot be successful if we do not know we have been successful. Standards define achievement and success.

In bowling, "300" is a perfect game. This is the standard of achievement.

In baseball, a "no hitter" is the perfect game. This is the standard of achievement.

In life, as in sports, we all need defined standards to aim at. We need to know how we are doing. A successful leader sets definable and measurable standards with subordinates. He/she allows mutual goal setting and then rewards achievement.

Success means winning consistently – not just winning once. A successful leader is continually successful. Somehow, he/she manages to turn failures into success, lemons into lemonade and success into more successes.

Set standards for success so people can know when they have succeeded.

FARANDA MAXIM

Bottoms Up Suggestions Are Useless... Without Top Down Actions.

People Care When They Know That Management Cares.

Toyota gets almost 2 million suggestions from its people every year. They get these suggestions because they ask for them and because they act on them. Every suggestion is acknowledged. Over 95% of the suggestions are implemented. The recognition as well as the financial remuneration is the reward.

The "C–L–A" Formula

People care when management **C**ares.

People care when management **L**istens.

People care when management **A**cts.

The bottom will stop sending ideas up when the top stops sending action down.

Management needs a symbiotic and not parasitic relationship with labor. Both sides must benefit from each other and not at the expense of one another.

Labor is a critical resource, not a variable cost.

People stop being an idea resource when they realize that management doesn't care about or use their ideas. Don't lose this critical resource.

Learn to Care.

Learn to Listen.

Learn to Act.

T
TEAMS

> *Teams Only Do Well*
> *When Individuals*
> *In The Teams Do Well.*

Teams are Like Family. They Don't Like Each Other All the Time, but They Must Still Work Together if They Want to Stay Together.
"T.E.A.M. =
Together Everyone Achieves More."
(Author Unknown)

Each member of the team must be achieving personal goals while the team achieves team goals if it is to be successful.

In western philosophy, the individual goal supersedes the team goal. (In America, we honor the "star" rather than the team.)

In eastern philosophy the team goal is the only goal. (In Japan, "the nail that is sticking up gets hammered down.")

Today, the western philosophy is moving east and the eastern philosophy is moving west.

We now acknowledge the importance of individual success within the team. We must not forget, however, to acknowledge the success of the team as a whole. We must also recognize the success of those who helped the "stars" to be successful.

O. J. Simpson never took credit for himself. He always gave credit to the team. He went the extra mile to acknowledge the front line people who helped him achieve his success. Then they went the extra mile to continue helping him be successful. The team won because individuals within the team won.

Teams only do well when individuals in the teams do well.

*Individuals Provide
A Narrow Assessment
Based On
A Limited Perspective.
Teams Provide
A Broad Assessment
Based On
An Overall Perspective.*

Learn to Use Teams When You Need the "Big Picture."

The three blind men and the elephant story is well-known. As each blind man touched a different part of the elephant, he described accurately what he was touching. Individually, however, none of the blind men described the total elephant. Collectively their descriptions added up to an elephant. Once again, the broad perspective of the team provided a more accurate assessment.

During the Bay of Pigs crisis, president J. F. Kennedy relied on only a few people for advice. They provided a narrow assessment based on a limited perspective. The Bay of Pigs was a disaster that almost ruined the Kennedy presidency.

During the Cuban missile crisis, JFK brought together a team of the best minds available. They succeeded. It was a broader assessment based on an overall perspective. He became a hero.

The same man, two different crisis situations, two different courses of action. The team assessment succeeded.

Teams work, use them.

T

TEAMS

Treat Your Team as Insiders Not Outsiders.

A Successful Organization is a Team: A Successful Group of Individuals Who Really Care.

A true team definition includes everyone involved in the process of creating, manufacturing, selling and delivering a product or service to the ultimate consumer.

Your team includes your employees, suppliers and customers.

Leaders who define their team in this fashion are more successful in reaching their organizational goals as well as their own personal goals.

Treating people as team-mates means sharing information and resources. It means hurting when they hurt and helping them to stop hurting. It means celebrating when things go well and commiserating when they don't. Team-mates really care about each other. Effective leaders show their team-mates that they care.

Treat your team as insiders, not outsiders.

FARANDA MAXIM

Make Sure the Technology is Justified by the ROI.

It is Easy to Go Broke Creating New Technology.

If you put knowledgeable people together with information, and give them unlimited resources, you will get technology. If you manage technology correctly, you will get a ROI (return on your investment).

The new technology, however, must be customer and market driven if it is to produce sufficient ROI to justify itself.

When Litton created the microwave oven it had to create not only a new technology, but a new market. Litton had to sell the *idea* of microwave as well as the *product* of microwave. Other firms who entered the market at a later date earned a higher ROI than Litton.

When Apple Computer created the personal computer they also had to create a market for the personal computer. Apple is one of the only original computer manufacturers who survived this new market when it crashed.

IBM never crashed. It waited until the market was more mature. Then, it entered the market. IBM's ROI on personal computers has been excellent.

Create technology. But remember the market and the price.

Technology without ROI is like a computer manufactured buggy whip in an era of space ships – nice to have but basically useless.

T

TASK FORCES

FARANDA MAXIM

> *People Hate Committees,*
> *People Like Task Forces.*

Substitute Task Forces for Committees.

A committee has unlimited life and undefined purpose. A task force has limited life and defined purpose.

Create task forces to solve specific problems. Legislate them out of existence after a preset period of time. Limit membership from three to five people. Make them responsible for results.

Stop using committees. They seldom work. People hate them. They live useless lives forever.

Start using task forces. They work. People like them. They live purposeful if short lives.

> FARANDA MAXIM
>
> *The Lone Ranger*
> *Never Helped Anyone*
> *In The Long Run.*

"High Ho, Silver and Away." "Who was that Masked Man Anyway?"

The Lone Ranger represents everything a successful leader should not be.

The Lone Ranger always solved the problem, but he never trained anyone else to solve it. He never built a team. He never provided solutions in his absence. He was a crisis solver, not a crisis preventor.

The Lone Ranger was a thumb in the dike and not a patch. When he was gone the dike could leak again. The dike wasn't fixed. It was just temporarily restrained.

A successful leader trains his/her team to be independent and interdependent. He/she cross trains people to be successful in more than one function. He/she develops a specific training plan for each person to help them grow and develop.

A successful leader is never a "Lone Ranger." He/she is a team leader.

Team leaders succeed in today's organizations, Lone Rangers do not.

T

TRAINING

In Four Hours You Can Learn How To Remove An Appendix.

It Will Take Four Years To Learn What To Do If Anything Goes Wrong.

Real Training is Knowing What to Do When Something Goes Wrong.

A surgeon's job during an appendectomy is routine – "by the numbers." A good surgeon today can complete an appendectomy in less than ten minutes. The surgeon's real skill is knowing what to do if something goes wrong.

A commercial pilot's job is "99% boredom and 1% sheer terror." All of their training is focused in that 1% of "terror time" when they must act immediately and correctly.

Real training is knowing what to do when something goes wrong.

Real training is knowing how to answer "what if" questions.

Train in depth. Train on contingency plans. Train on credibility. Train on action not re-action.

Train – test – retrain. Then train again.

You can never overtrain a person in the changing world of today.

An undertrained person in today's world is an organization's biggest liability.

Training is an investment not a cost.

> FARANDA MAXIM
>
> *Training
> Is Tomorrow's
> Precious Metal*

People Who Refuse Training Refuse Success in Life.

Get all the training you can. Never refuse an opportunity to learn. Every new thing you learn increases both your self confidence and your value in the marketplace.

In today's changing world, you can become technologically obsolescent very fast.

Training is the only cure for technological obsolescence.

Once you have mastered a skill it is yours forever. No employer can ever take it from you. You have given yourself a gift of the greatest value.

"The only thing more expensive than education is ignorance."

Ben Franklin

Treat your training like gold in your safe deposit box.

Training is tomorrow's precious metal. Acquire it. Use it. Store it. Insure it. Training yourself today is your future tomorrow.

T
TRADITION

A Wise Leader Knows When To Substitute New Traditions For Old Ones.

Effective Leaders Understand the Bonding Concept of Tradition. Tradition Is the Glue That Holds Organizations Together. A Poor Leader Lets the Glue Harden.

Black & Decker knew that they had to make a major cultural change to continue as one of the world's power tool leaders. To accomplish this they had to establish new traditions to replace those that were no longer applicable. In 1985-86 they made their major moves. Sales went up. Profits went up. ROI went up. They are a world leader.

New traditions are like new caulk. They replace the old caulk that has hardened and cracked. New caulk is flexible and seals out the elements.

Tradition, at its best, is a bonding mechanism to provide security and stability. At its worst, tradition is an inhibitor that prevents change and innovation.

Successful leaders know when and how to substitute new traditions for old ones. They know which traditions are "bonders" and which are "inhibitors."

A wise leader knows when to substitute new traditions for old ones.

V

VISION

Leader Myopia is a Fatal Disease.

Sears has been seeing nearsighted through rose coloured glasses. Because of it, they have had to try to sell their "Sears Tower" headquarters in Chicago.

Leader myopia will do that to you.

Sometimes the ivory tower is a jail that locks everyone else out. Ideas cannot scale the walls or swim the moat through the alligators. Eventually, the ivory tower yellows and loses its lustre.

A vision is a realistic view of the way you want things to be. It is a picture of the future based on the past and present. It is a kaleidoscope of resources that are clearly in focus.

Successful corporations of all sizes have a vision. It is written down. Everyone in the organization understands it and has it memorized. All planning is centered around it. The vision provides direction.

"USA Today" had a vision of being the largest selling daily newspaper in America – of beating the "Wall Street Journal." They reached their goal because everyone knew this was a top priority for the future. All decisions were centered on achieving this. It provided all employees clarity of thought and action. It provided purpose.

A vision is a lovely thing to look at. It puts results on paper and money in your pocket.

V

VALUES

Values Provide Security.
Make Sure Values Represent
Growth Not Paralysis.

A Written Vision and Values Statement is Critical to Growing an Organization Profitably.

Values drive attitudes and behavior. Behavior is a function of attitude. Attitude is a function of values.

We believe. We think. We act.

A written organizational values statement tells everyone what top management believes, how it thinks, how it will behave.

A person without values is doomed to failure. He/she has no support post to lean on.

A corporation without values is an empty shell dedicated to making money rather than to solving needs and problems.

Both can survive. Neither can flourish.

Values are like engine block supports. They get little attention until they break down. They are critical but not noticeable. They absorb all the vibrations and still keep the engine intact. No one thanks them.

If your motor is racing, but you are getting nowhere fast, look at your engine block supports. They might need a little shoring up.

WAGES

Customers are the source of all prosperity

Customers are the most ignored partners in the organization. We expect them to do their part – buy our products and services. We expect them to strengthen our cash flow. We expect them to return time after time ... with a smile on their face and money in their hand.

Most corporate managers do not even know their top fifty customers by name. They do not really know what their customers produce or how they do it. They do not know who their customer's suppliers are. Or who their customer's customers are.

What they often know is less relevant to a long term relationship than what they do not know. Some are so ignorant they do not know that they do not know.

Know everything about your customers. Know everything about their customers, suppliers, products, services, needs, wants, problems, abilities, strengths, weaknesses and capabilities.

If you do not take the time to know your customers ... someone else will!

> "The employer doesn't pay the wages. The customer pays the wages. The employer only handles the money."
>
> (Henry Ford)

Y

YESTERDAY

Yesterday Is To Today
As
Today Is To Tomorrow.

Live For the Moment
Lest You Lose It.

We Have Always Had a "Yesterday." We are Now Having a "Today." There is No Guarantee We Will Have a "Tomorrow."

Each moment of time is a gift that will not be repeated. Learn to accept and use the gift – it may not be offered when you are ready for it.

When you cannot remember one significant accomplishment from today it means you have lost that day.

You can only make up a day by crossing the international date line. However, you have to lose one first.

It is easy to live for tomorrow. What is hard is to live for today.

The gift of today is precious. It is not a commodity. It is not a promise of more to come. It is simply one more day by which your life has been shortened (or lengthened). If your life was shortened by joy and happiness then your day was "invested" into your life. If your day was shortened by conflict and controversy then your day was "spent" from your life.

Life is a sacred treasure. Lock it up. Insure it. Live it. Love it.

Once the treasure is gone, the chest is empty.

Invest your life. Don't just spend it.

> ### FARANDA MAXIM
>
> *A Zero Defects Program*
> *Is Part Of A*
> *Quality Program.*
> *Focus On Quality And*
> *You'll Get Zero Defects.*

Zero Defect is a Manufacturing Philosophy. Quality is a Total Organizational Philosophy.

Few zero defect programs have been effective without total quality programs to back them. A total quality program involves everyone – from manufacturing to order processing to statistical process control to management.

Quality is not a management program – it is a way of life. Quality must be accepted by every person at every level of the organization.

> "The quality goal is to be so good that your customer has no reason to change."
>
> (T. W. Faranda)

Ford has increased its market share ever since installing a total quality program. The Ford Taurus automobile was the start of an entire new way of manufacturing automobiles - featuring quality as a product benefit and value and not a feature. At Ford, everyone is taught that quality is their number one priority. It has paid off.

> "Quality is remembered long after price is forgotten."
>
> (Author Unknown)

Quality doesn't cost, it pays. Successful leaders and organizations know this and act accordingly.

Quality doesn't cost, it pays.

Z

ZERO BASED BUDGETING

There is Usually a Little Extra Air in the Pie Dough. Roll it Out.

Managers are masters at documenting the need for budgetary increases for their departments. They usually ask for more than they expect to get knowing they will get less than they ask for.

This vicious cycle never addresses the basic question: how well are you using the resources you have already?

Forcing a manager to justify, on a yearly basis, the entire amount of his/her budget – from a base of $0 – forces a showdown at the OK Coral. It is either shoot or be shot. They may do a great job of justifying the increase but fail to validate the base budget they now operate under. Zero based budgeting often reduces what you must give managers to operate and often generates just as many results.

Zero based budgeting is an investment in time and effort. It brings back a strong "ROI" (Return on Investment) and helps department or SBU heads to understand the contribution they must make to the organization as a whole.

Invest in this technique and you will see the difference. It makes good horse sense to get in the habit of closing the barn door before the horses get out.